ANTHONY TROLLOPE

A NEW JUDGEMENT

ANTHONY TROLLOPE

ANTHONY TROLLOPE

A New Judgement

BY ELIZABETH BOWEN

1946

Oxford University Press

New York & London

ILLUSTRATIONS

ANTHONY TROLLOPE

A NEW JUDGEMENT

ANTHONY TROLLOPE

NARRATOR [*in level, descriptive voice*]: The walls are lined with books. On their backs, the firelight should be playing—but this is wartime: there is an electric radiator, with one bar lit, in the grate. As close as possible to the radiator, the study's owner reclines in an armchair. A fastidious, pleasant, elderly man. He is lost to the world, reading. He holds the book in long fingers. The door opens. A young man in battle-dress hesitates on the threshold before speaking.

WILLIAM: Uncle Jasper?

UNCLE JASPER [*startled*]: Who's that? Why, William! [*warmly*] William . . . Come in, come in, dear boy!

WILLIAM: Disturbing you?

UNCLE JASPER: I like it. Pull up that other chair. Cigarette?

WILLIAM [*in uncertain voice*]: Thanks, I . . .

[3]

UNCLE JASPER: Settle down, dear boy, settle down.

WILLIAM: Actually, I haven't got too much time. [*significantly*] Got a train to catch.

UNCLE JASPER [*vaguely*]: Train? [*change of tone—gravely*] Oh. You mean—you're off?

WILLIAM: Very soon—yes.

UNCLE JASPER: One does not ask where?

WILLIAM: We-ell . . .

UNCLE JASPER: But one makes a pretty good guess?

WILLIAM [*audibly grinning*]: One makes a pretty good guess.

UNCLE JASPER [*in tone of controlled feeling*]: Well, I'm glad you looked in, you know: it was nice of you.

WILLIAM [*inarticulate*]: Well, I mean to say . . . [*pause, with audible grin again*] Besides, I wanted to ask—

UNCLE JASPER [*quickly, pleased*]: What—anything *I* can do?

WILLIAM: Well, it's quite a thing to ask—[*with a rush*] Can I take a book?

UNCLE JASPER [*with instinctive reluctance*]: Take a book *away?*

WILLIAM: Well, it comes to that. . . . It *is* quite a thing to ask. And I don't want any old book; I want a Trollope. You know—Anthony Trollope.

UNCLE JASPER [*ironical*]: I know: Anthony Trollope.

WILLIAM: You don't think much of him?

UNCLE JASPER: He doesn't say much to me. That may be my fault: I'm not saying it's not. God forbid *I* should run down any honest man who gives honest pleasure. In fact, who has done so twice. He pleased his own generation—and so he should have done: he had got them taped. And, which seems a good deal odder, he pleases yours—I wish you could tell me why. *I* belong to the generation halfway between: in fact, by a funny coincidence, I was born the year Trollope died — 1882. And frankly, William, by the time I was your age, which is to say in the early nineteen-hundreds, Trollope was so stone dead, so utterly off the map, that he might just as well not have been born at all. He'd outstayed his welcome, with his most devoted readers; his reputation went with him down to the grave.

[5]

WILLIAM [*thoughtful*]: Funny . . . [*brightening*] It didn't stay there.

UNCLE JASPER [*absently*]: No . . . [*energetically*] Trollope died—in both senses—at the time when the English novel was coming into its own. Hardy, Meredith, Henry James were all in the field. Trollope—by his own admission—wrote for young ladies. Hardy, Meredith, James, wrote for adult minds; or at least, for minds that wanted to be adult. It may seem odd to you, William—in fact, I say this to you with some humility—but we young men, when *I* was a young man, surrounded as we were, to the outward eye, with all the good things of those piping times of peace, *did* look on life as a psychological battle. And into that battle we took our three novelists—Hardy, Meredith, James. Yes, those were the great names when I was your age. And frankly, where I am concerned, they're the great names still. And now? I see *you* go into actual battle carrying Trollope!

WILLIAM [*simply*]: I like him.

UNCLE JASPER: Wherefore, I take off my hat to him. *Not* as a novelist—that would be asking too much.

Yes, I *have* tried one or two of his books these last few years, but I couldn't away with any of them. Plum duff, sheer plum duff! No, no, no, no—Henry James, as generous a critic as you wish, said about all for Trollope that could be said, in that essay on him in *Partial Portraits* . . . 'Strong, genial, abundant' . . . 'Something masterly in his large-fisted grip' . . . 'He represents to an admirable degree the natural decorum of the English spirit' . . . 'His complete appreciation of the ordinary' . . . Yes, that—all that. It took James's fine eye to see it. But he, even he, was forced to the last conclusion—and for him, as for me, it *was* the damning one—'Trollope's imagination had no light of its own.'

WILLIAM: And yet—you take off your hat to him?

UNCLE JASPER [*smile in voice*]: There must be *something* about any writer who lives twice. He's a double man. There's the Trollope his own generation knew, and the Trollope yours has found—or, perhaps, created?

WILLIAM: Created?

UNCLE JASPER: You don't think you give him something he hadn't got?

[7]

WILLIAM: I do think he's got something we've never had.

UNCLE JASPER [*reflective, struck*]: That's possible. Something you would have liked? Come to that, old Trollope immortalizes quite a few things I could do with myself. [*shivers*] On a day like *this*, I could do with one of those Plumstead Episcopi roaring fires. . . . The rooks in the elms, the port on the table. . . . [*abruptly*] Which do you want?

WILLIAM [*uncertain*]: Which?——

UNCLE JASPER: Which of the Trollope novels?

WILLIAM [*much relieved*]: Oh, you *have* got some of him, then? I began to wonder.

UNCLE JASPER [*dryly*]: If you move that sofa—which will involve moving the table first—I think you'll find three or four away in the corner, down on the bottom shelf. [*more dryly*] They were your great-aunt Emily's.

WILLIAM [*to sound of moving sofa*]: That old war-horse? Fancy me and Aunt Emily seeing with the same eye! [*pause: voice muffled, as from corner of book-shelves*] Yes, here we are . . .

UNCLE JASPER [*reflective*]: With far from the same eye. Aunt Emily wanted the testimonial——

WILLIAM: Testimonial——

UNCLE JASPER: To her own way of living. Whereas, you want——

WILLIAM [*amused*]: What do *I* want?

UNCLE JASPER: A picture book?

WILLIAM: A picture book . . . [*amused*] Well, I'll look at it in the train.

UNCLE JASPER: Very proper—he probably wrote it in the train.

🖝 *Pause: Fade-in train noises—rather accentuated. as of train taking up-gradient. Gradually fade in, on top of these noises and in their rhythm, voice saying 'A picture book, a picture book, a picture book' . . . The words should gain, slowly, more with each time of speaking, over train noises.*

🖝 *Both Faded Out.*

NARRATOR: William is very tired. He has had quite a day, saying so many good-byes in a short time. Kit

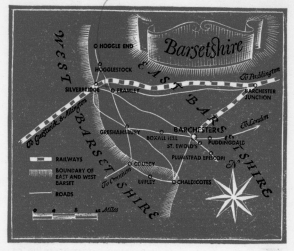

stowed in the rack above him, he is dozing, arms folded, in a corner of the compartment—which is surprisingly empty. The book he was holding has slipped to the seat beside him. The mists of William's drowsiness clear and thin as, from time to time, he opens his eyes. Lit by bland winter afternoon sunshine, a landscape streams past the windows. A stone house with white window-frames, basking in the yellow light of a valley . . . A church spire . . .

[10]

A man on horseback, trotting on the grass verge of a road . . . The lichened roofs of farm buildings . . . In the distance—the smoke of a little city, turned by the sun to gauze . . . And, rising above this— surely?—cathedral towers . . . Now, which cathedral can *that* be?

TROLLOPE [*a very deep voice, at once genial and diffident*]: Barchester, sir.

NARRATOR [*as though surprised*]: William must have slept through the stop at the last station. For, he finds, the seat opposite him, empty last time he looked, is now occupied. A big, clumsy man, with a bushy square beard, sits there, eyeing him over thick spectacles that have slipped some way down on his nose.

WILLIAM [*bewildered*]: This country we're going through—it's familiar. Yet I can't, somehow, place it.

TROLLOPE: Possibly not on the map; no, possibly not on the map. [*with detachment, after clearing throat*] A new shire I added to the English counties.

WILLIAM [*automatically*]: Really sir? [*apologetic laugh*] I'm afraid I'm not very bright today.

[11]

TROLLOPE: Much on your mind, no doubt? Well, well. Youth is never an easy time. Not for much would I live through my own again.

WILLIAM: If you'll excuse me, sir, you're the first person of—of anything like *your* age that I've ever heard say that!

TROLLOPE: Oh, heaven endows a number of us old fellows with remarkably kind, false memories. That wasn't so in my case. No, all through my good years —and they were many, for my turning-point came when I was twenty-seven; and I lived to be sixty-eight—I was liable, any night, to wake up sweating from the nightmare that I was young again. Idleness, inferiority, envy. The seamy side. Those are the things, you know, that you don't forget. They don't have to cripple you: they didn't cripple me. But it takes the rest of your remaining days to get up with what they have done to you. Let's say they give you, and leave you with, one particular manner of seeing life. You continue to see life that way, whatever comes. Yes, whatever comes. [*pause*] Industry, success, popularity, well-being. . . . The strong, well-lit desk and my pen flowing well ahead

[12]

of the clock. . . . The peaches and roses in the garden; my boys' voices out there—my boys had a happy youth. . . . Cheques rolling in, bills paid, the bank balance mounting up. The dinner parties— oh, those dinner parties of the 'eighties!

☞ *Fade In*

FIRST LADY [*against general background of tinkling glass, laughter and conversation—her voice flattering, arch*]: Now, Mr. Trollope, you wonderful, naughty man, I've got something ever so *serious* to say to you. You really *must* let Lily Dale marry Johnnie Eames! Agatha and I would be *heartbroken*. . . .

SECOND LADY [*more fluttering*]: Mr. Trollope, may I just ask you this? I have quite a favourite uncle who's an archdeacon, and he's astounded by your knowledge of clergymen. *I* said that perhaps your father was an archbishop?

FIRST LADY: In confidence—I so wonder—*has* your Lady Glencora any original in real life?

SECOND LADY: One can but blame her, of course— though [*wistfully*] Burgo Fitzgerald was *very* fascinating! [*increasingly daring*] Come, Mr. Trollope, I know you will never tell me, but how *do* you know so much about ladies' hearts?

FIRST LADY: And peers?

SECOND LADY: And politics?

FIRST LADY: And, even—*quite—low—life?*

☞ *Fade Out*

TROLLOPE [*reflective*]: My glass refilled, camellias, charming bright eyes, warming rustle of silks. And, dearest prospect of all, my return home. . . . And those evenings at the Garrick—of which I became a member in '61. Having up to that time lived very little among men—having hitherto been banished from social gatherings—I enjoyed infinitely the gaiety of the Garrick: it was a festival to me to dine there. [*pause—very modestly*] I think that I became popular among those with whom I associated. I had long, for very long, been aware of a certain weakness in my own character, which I may call a craving for love. The Garrick Club was the first assemblage of men. . . .

☞ *Fade Out*

☞ Fade-in sounds of men's voices, laughter: A generally prosperous and port-winey background of sound, with a confident Bohemian animation.

FIRST MAN: Ha, ha—very good—excellent. Tell Thackeray.

SECOND MAN [*cutting in*]: You forget, the best of it was, that *The Times* next day. . . .

THIRD MAN [*very cordial*]: Aha—*here* comes the real good fellow. Evening, Trollope.

ALL [*to sound of chairs being pushed back*]: Hello! Evening! Anything new? Was feeling *you* were about due in. Things going on well? Needless to ask *you* that! Dirty evening, out there. Come to the fire. Last come, first served. Whist—bring the table up. Look, Trollope, before you get down to whist—tell me this, Trollope . . . Trollope . . . Listen to this, Trollope . . . (*etc.*).

☞ Fade-out Garrick

☞ Fade-in subdued train sounds.

[15]

TROLLOPE [*picking up from point where voice left off*]: The first assemblage of men at which I felt myself to be popular.

WILLIAM [*resigned to the oddness of this, but thoughtful*]: You *are* Anthony Trollope?

TROLLOPE: Well, yes—I know myself by that name. [*pause*] I know myself, that's to say, at least not less well than I know my characters.

WILLIAM [*taken aback*]: Isn't that, sir, a funny way round to put it? Surely one more often hears an author say that he knows his characters almost as well as he knows himself?

TROLLOPE: Indeed? Then you must know some clever fellows. No—[*reflective pause*] It's been t'other way round with me. I've thought more about my characters than I have about myself. To be honest, I like 'em a good deal better. I much prefer their company to my own. For my own company, first, I had no taste—misery, loneliness, wretchedness thrust me into it. I'd escape from it at any moment I could—into daydreams, in which I was a quite different fellow. It was that, no doubt, that set up my first habit of spinning yarns.

WILLIAM [*thoughtful*]: But later, sir, once you'd got thoroughly launched, once you'd got a name, once you had started to do so well?

TROLLOPE: Oh, by then I had no time for my own company, I was a busy man—organized down to each moment of every day. I had a lot to get through, and I got through it. [*simply*] I was a happy man. And a happy, busy man isn't given to thinking about himself. That's an idler's trick—and a wretched, unhappy trick, if you ask me.

WILLIAM [*still perplexed*]: Still, *I* always did understand that all writers, from Shakespeare down, drew their characters out of what they knew of themselves. If that was not so in your case, where *did* your people come from? Archdeacon Grantly, Plantagenet Palliser, old Mr. Harding—to mention only a few. Heaven knows, they're foursquare and alive enough!

TROLLOPE: Oh, yes, they're alive all right. [*chuckles*] A sight more alive than I am! [*reflective pause, then vaguely*] Oh, they came along, you know; they just came along. . . .

WILLIAM: But, out of *where?*

[17]

TROLLOPE [*with genuine piety*]: Ask the Almighty, my boy. No sense in asking me. I put myself into the habit of steady and rapid writing, set myself to turn out a set number of pages daily—and, moreover, turned 'em out, every day. That being so, my people just—came along.

WILLIAM: You suggest, you know, that a novelist is a sort of medium. Sits down, takes up his pen, goes into a sort of trance——

TROLLOPE [*cuts in—shocked*]: What—spirits? That flimmery-flummery? God forbid!

WILLIAM [*eager, pursuing his own idea*]: Or, better still, a sort of receiving station—picking up and transmitting all sorts of things that are in the air?

TROLLOPE [*not shocked now, merely dubious*]: Oh well, there, you know, we're outside my province. I had —er . . . left England . . . before any of *that* came in. Still, from what I've been able to see—and I watch with interest—there might—'pon my word, there might—be something in what you say. [*reflective pause*] Scenes, places, people yes, as I sat there writing, I saw them as sharply as though they *were* going on.

WILLIAM: And so, perhaps, they were, sir?

TROLLOPE [*still dubious; growling*]: Well, I don't know, I'm sure. [*sharply*] Mind, I'm not saying I didn't use my head. It may not have been a bright head, but it was a steady one. I worked out my plot at the start; I stuck to it—and, by Gad, I made the pack of 'em stick to it, what is more!

WILLIAM: Pack of whom?

TROLLOPE: The characters. Once or twice, one or two of 'em kicked their heels up, took ideas into their own heads. Sometimes, the ladies were the devil—as ladies can be the devil in real life. There were chapters, for instance, where I had a bit of trouble with that fine young widow, Eleanor Bold. Yes, writing a novel, my boy, is like driving pigs to market—you have one of them making a bolt down the wrong lane; another won't get over the right stile . . . However [*satisfied sigh*] we all got home in the end.

WILLIAM [*suddenly*]: Sir? May I be a bit impertinent?

TROLLOPE [*with unworried chuckle*]: Go on, my boy, go on.

[19]

WILLIAM: Well, you said just now—I don't know if you'll remember—that you knew yourself not less well than you knew your characters. You *then* proceeded to say that, first, you'd fled from yourself as from poison; and that, later on, you'd had no time for yourself. In that case—here's where I'm being impertinent—I don't see how you *can* know yourself at all.

TROLLOPE [*undisturbed*]: Yet I do, you know, yet I do. Yes, I know Anthony Trollope, for what he's worth. I kept learning about myself from my own characters. Some say that to be a father's an education—you may quite often recognize, in your children, bits of yourself you had never known were there. In the same way—and I should say even more so—I found it an education to be a novelist. My characters—the best of them, that's to say— were all more definite, more sure of themselves, more active, and—where they *were* admirable— more admirable than *I*, myself, had ever been in real life. [*chuckles*] My characters fairly marched in on me—took a look round, took stock, and made use of all that *I* had. Ah, they were cool hands.

[20]

[*chuckles again*] They commandeered me—my pen, my reasoning powers. And, more than that, they drew on a lot in me—desires, scruples, aspirations, and daydreams—of whose existence *I* had not been aware.

WILLIAM: They stole a march on you?

TROLLOPE [*resignedly*]: Put it that way. [*pause*] The best of them were what, without knowing, I should have liked to be. The worst of them—in the moral sense, that's to say—were what, without knowing, I'd somehow avoided being. My Warden, for instance—old Mr. Harding, in the novel, was a personification of my own muddled wish to do right at any cost. Plantagenet Palliser—the political hero whose career reaches its climax in my *Prime Minister* —is not only my political ideal, but personifies my own lost political hopes. I did once, you know, stand for Parliament: at the Beverley elections; I took a sickening knock, and from then on, I buried *my* hopes for ever. But from then on, also, Plantagenet Palliser grew. [*pause: sigh*] Well, well. . . . Who was the third you said?

WILLIAM [*eager*]: Archdeacon Grantly.

TROLLOPE [*between sigh and chuckle*]: The Archdeacon . . . A bad, bad man—over-ambitious, hard, self-important, in love with power? A decent fellow, loyal to those he loved, humane, even kindly, in some situations, just? . . . I can pass no judgement, you know, on the Archdeacon. He was the product of my moral consciousness. He raised, for me, questions *I* haven't answered yet.

WILLIAM: I suppose he cared for the world too much.

TROLLOPE [*after reflection, humbly*]: I cannot say *I* never cared for the world. . . . [*with return of confidence*] And I do say, I'd have been a fool if I hadn't.

WILLIAM: For me, it's not quite so simple. My world's in rather a mess.

TROLLOPE: So I understand. You are off to the wars, I see. Off to one of the fronts. War's everywhere— every place that you look.

WILLIAM [*impulsively*]: Do you know, Uncle Jasper says that's why so many people like me are reading your books again? He thinks—at least, I suspect he thinks so—that we're homesick for anything right-and-tight. The whole way of life that this country

[23]

outside the windows—this country we're running through now—suggests. The whole way of life that is quite, apparently, gone. When he let me take one of your books from his shelves just now, sir, he said —I hope you won't mind?—that I wanted a picture book.

TROLLOPE [*as though leaning forward*]: And you—*was* that what you wanted, eh?

WILLIAM: No, you know, he was wrong! Of course I *do* like, we all like, pictures of the old happy times————

TROLLOPE [*dubious*]: Altogether happy?

WILLIAM: Decent, at any rate. But I don't think, with us, that's the root of the thing. No. I think your novels are a support against the sort of *hopelessness* we're inclined to feel. As you say, the characters in your books are *active*. They keep on the move; and they make decisions. They know what they want, and they want what they want all out. If they don't get it they put such a good face on it, or keep such a flag flying, one is left to feel that they *have* won out, by the end. Your people are stronger than circumstances. Yes, I think I've got to the root of it—*that*

[24]

must be what we're after in your books. It's essential for us, these days, to believe in people, and in their power to live. Not just in heroes or monsters, but in ordinary people with the knack of living ordinary lives. Now, all of your characters, Mr. Trollope— except one or two of the monsters like Mrs. Proudie —were ordinary, in a way that sticks out a mile. And you see, we long for what's ordinary.

TROLLOPE: So did I.

WILLIAM: You, sir? But——?

TROLLOPE: How else could I have painted the ordinary in such sublime colours? Can't you see, my brush was tipped, from the first, with a desire that I could not forget? War isolates *you*, my friend, for the time being, from your proper inheritance as a young Englishman. In my own youth, I knew the same isolation—and that its reasons were different, only made it more bitter. [*shamed half-laugh*] I was a gentleman's son who was, apparently, never to be a gentleman, and who knew of no way to be anything else. My father, consuming himself as he consumed our fortunes, remorselessly confronted me with an ideal which I could not approach. For my failure—

Aug 8 ············· by whom
168 ············· get hold of the amusing
····· and, more ······· everybody consigned ·········
····· such ······· ? ········· Will I ever
so unblushed ······· like the ··········· of a punch with
a ······· ········· to satisfy the ever ········· of
New York ······ ·················
········ Stores the ········ together with him
offence, and he ······ his ········ of the ·······
········ ······· to the ······ ; he ······· a fault I have
······· in the presence of such a ······ I am hardened,
········ ·············

Of Framley Parsonage I need only further say that
(240) as I wrote it I became more closely acquainted than ever with
the new shire which I had added to the English counties. I
had it all in my mind, its roads, and railroads its towns
and parishes, its members of Parliament, and the different
hunts which rode over it. I knew all the great lords and
their castles, the squires and their parks, the rectors and
their churches. This was the fourth novel of which I had
placed the scene in Barsetshire, and as I wrote it I
made a map of the dear county. Throughout these stories
there has been no name given to a fictitious site, which
does not represent to me a spot of which I know all the accessories,
as though I had lived and wandered there.

which had been his failure—he hated me and made me hate myself. He was at pains to place me where I should suffer most—I enjoyed, I believe, the unique distinction of being miserable—a butt, a failure—at *two* of the greatest English Public Schools. At the two great schools, my father's story was known—disclosed by his failure to pay my fees. All those years I was surrounded by school-fellows who enjoyed what I should have had—who were poised, successful, assured. Could I fail to romanticize those other lives, those other futures, so unlike mine? At eighteen, I was a shambling usher at a poor school in Belgium. At nineteen, I was a clerk in the Post Office. Yes, in time, I respectably worked my way up; but those first years in the Post Office were —well, well . . . Idleness, debts and squalor, interludes of too well-deserved disgrace. And all that—can't you see it?—made ten times worse by my mirages, my dream-pictures of other lives, built up out of those glimpses that I had had?

WILLIAM [*slightly bewildered*]: I'm sorry, sir.

TROLLOPE [*sharply*]: Thanks, I don't ask for pity. I **was merely—explaining.** [*pause*] How, once, I

[27]

yearned for the ordinary like a lover. How I came to depict cheerful, confident people, serene homes, honoured positions, as a lover might depict his beloved's face. However, however . . . [*lapse into sudden embarrassment—then abruptly, with complete change of tone*] May I ask which of my novels you've got there?

WILLIAM: *The Small House at Allington.*

TROLLOPE: Eh? My old eyes may deceive me, sir, but I *think* you'll find you are wrong.

WILLIAM: Surely? . . . [*pause, then outcry*] Oh, gosh— *oh* gosh! This would happen to *me*! Wrong book! That bottom shelf was dark; and I was in a hurry. Here I am, now, stuck for the duration with some mouldy old autobiography!

TROLLOPE [*dryly*]: Mine, I think.

WILLIAM [*flustered*]: Yours, sir? I'd no idea . . .

TROLLOPE [*with amused defiance*]: Well, I did. I wrote one. Cannot regret it, either: did me the world of good. Of course, ruined me, finished my good name. I'd left it with my son Henry, for posthumous pub-

[28]

lication, so he brought it out the year after I'd—
left the scene. Yes, my poor lad Henry, he had to
face the music: I felt bad about that—otherwise, I
had a hearty laugh!

WILLIAM [*puzzled, diffident*]: Was it—er—scandalous,
sir?

TROLLOPE [*chuckling*]: Scandalously honest! Or so it
seemed to the lot who read it when it came out:
1883, you know—they were just beginning to have
fine feelings. Felt that writers ought to be artists,
and so on. Made 'em wince. My own lot, I think,
would have understood—Thackeray, for instance;
but he'd gone on ahead. And *your* lot, in its turn, I
feel somehow, may understand. In fact, my boy,
may I say there's no book of mine I would rather
see you take with you to the battle? Read it, will
you?—and *then* go back to the novels. Maybe I
wrote it for you. It's the truth—or as near the truth
as man ever came.

WILLIAM: Sir—[*no answer*] Mr. Trollope! [*slightly
frantic*] Sir! [*pause—bemused voice*] He's—he's not—
Have I been asleep then? It's getting dark . . .

☛ *Fade-in train noises for a few seconds, in same rhythm as before, accompanied by voice saying 'The Ordinary! The Ordinary—The Ordinary . . .'*

☛ *Fade Out*

NARRATOR: Yes, it is getting dark. One can just see that the seat opposite William is no longer occupied —if it ever was. Outside the carriage windows the winter country is fading, flowing into the dusk. Perhaps, indeed, we have crossed the Barset border and are back in the numbered English counties again. The sunshine, timeless, mellow, and bland, that fell on Trollope's spires and roofs and roads and manorial gates is gone.

UNCLE JASPER'S VOICE [*as though quoting*]: 'Trollope's imagination had no light of its own.'

NARRATOR: No: only genius sheds light. Faithful talent receives the plain light of nature, holds it, reflects it back. Trollope holds up a mirror in which English faces, seasons, and scenes remain. It is a mirror, not distorting, not flattering; with only one magic quality—retention. Can one wonder it should reassure William to look across the years, and find,

[30]

in the Trollope mirror, faces so like his own? [*pause*] It was not the clumsy and grubby boy, or the seedy clerk, that the world remembered. The big, burly, genial, likeable chap; the unflagging, successful author; the esteemed Civil Servant; the hard rider to hounds; the prosaically happy husband and father—this was the image left. This was the image that was, in time, to bore Uncle Jasper and his more finely strung generation. *Were* there two Trollopes? Uncle Jasper, off-hand, has thrown us out the idea. The anxious outcast, the successful man of the world—was the first, perhaps, never quite absorbed and lost in the second? Is it the wistful outsider, somewhere in Trollope's writing, who gives that mirage-illusion to the ordinary scene?

Is it the mirage that William seeks? . . .

Yes, it is dark in the railway carriage. The train bears on to his destination William, now sleeping deeply, without a dream—head dropped forward over his folded arms. The *Autobiography* has slipped from his hold again—this time, to the floor. The pages blow over rapidly, in a draught. So the last paragraph is exposed for a moment—it is too dark to read it . . .

[31]

TROLLOPE'S VOICE [*from the distance and with a solemn impersonality*]: 'Now I stretch out my hand and from the further shore I bid adieu to all who have cared to read the many words I have written.' . . . Now I stretch out my hand . . .

BIBLIOGRAPHY

(not including the travel books and miscellaneous writings)

1847.   The Macdermots of Ballycloran
1848.   The Kellys and the O'Kellys*
1850.   La Vendée
1855.   The Warden*†
1857.   Barchester Towers*†
1858.   The Three Clerks*
1858.   Doctor Thorne*†
1859.   The Bertrams
1860.   Castle Richmond
1861.   Framely Parsonage*†
1861.   Tales of All Countries: First Series*
1862.   Orley Farm*
1863.   Tales of All Countries: Second Series
1863.   Rachel Ray*
1864.   The Small House at Allington*†
1864.   Can You Forgive Her?*
1865.   Miss Mackenzie*
1866.   The Belton Estate*
1867.   Nina Balatka*

1867.   The Last Chronicle of Barset*†

1867.   The Claverings*

1867.   Lotta Schmidt and Other Stories

1868.   Linda Tressel*

1869.   Phineas Finn*

1869.   He Knew He Was Right*

1870.   The Vicar of Bullhampton*

1870.   An Editor's Tales

1870.   The Struggles of Brown, Jones and Robinson

1871.   Sir Harry Hotspur of Humblethwaite*

1871.   Ralph the Heir*

1872.   The Golden Lion of Grandpère*

1873.   The Eustace Diamonds*

1874.   Phineas Redux†

1874.   Lady Anna*

1874.   Harry Heathcote of Gangoil

1875.   The Way We Live Now*

1876.   The Prime Minister*

1877.   The American Senator*

1878.   Is He Popenjoy?*

1879.   An Eye for an Eye

1879.   John Caldigate*

1879.   Cousin Henry*

1880.   The Duke's Children*

1881. Dr. Wortle's School*

1881. Ayala's Angel*

1882. Why Frau Frohmann Raised Her Prices, and Other Stories

1882. Kept in the Dark

1882. Marion Fay

1882. The Fixed Period

Issued Posthumously

1883. Mr. Scarborough's Family*

1883. The Landleaguers

1883. An Autobiography*

1884. An Old Man's Love*

* Included in 'The World's Classics' series (Oxford University Press).

† These works constitute the Barsetshire Novels.

Anthony Trollope was designed by John Begg
and printed by L. F. White Company, Inc.
The binding and lettering were done by
Wolf Eckardt: Frontispiece and map wood
engravings by Hans Jelinek.